Late P

Also by Gavin Selerie:

Playground for the Working Line (Ziesing Brothers, 1981)
Azimuth (Binnacle Press, 1984)
Puzzle Canon (Spectacular Diseases, 1986)
Strip Signals (Galloping Dog Press, 1986)
Elizabethan Overhang (Spectacular Diseases, 1989)
Southam Street (New River Project, 1991)
Tilting Square (Binnacle Press, 1992)
Roxy (West House Books, 1996)
Danse Macabre, with Alan Halsey et al
          (Ispress & West House Books, 1997)
Days of '49, with Alan Halsey (West House Books, 1999)
Vitagraph (Binnacle Press, 2001)
Le Fanu's Ghost (Five Seasons Press, 2006)
The Canting Academy, with David Annwn et al (Ispress, 2008)
Music's Duel. New and Selected Poems 1972–2008
          (Shearsman Books, 2009)
Hariot Double (Five Seasons Press, 2016)
Collected Sonnets (Shearsman Books, 2019)

Late Poems

Gavin Selerie

Shearsman Books

First published in the United Kingdom in 2024 by
Shearsman Books
P.O. Box 4239
Swindon
SN3 9FN

Shearsman Books Ltd Registered Office
30–31 St. James Place, Mangotsfield, Bristol BS16 9JB
(this address not for correspondence)

www.shearsman.com

ISBN 978-1-84861-951-7

Contents

1. Pandemic Poems

Biocalypse

Staring crags in the mirror, would Wystan
have lathered and scrubbed his hands
to defy the joker who'd climb into your lungs
and squeeze your skull? Say Mars has turned his face
to earth and marched into a cell
unpestered with people, gifting germs on a writer's
finger, would you wipe those invisible dots
and sleep in a glass bed under glass sheets?
Through queasy time we picture a bat in a far-off cave
that has in its folds some spirit may spike
a protein under scales of what makes meat
in a sloshed market—taken, passed
down global tracks aired in or sailed out
to get over and over as too late a masterless face
tries to close the grid, a grunting girgashite
elected at a leaky border the fist and glove
won't steel. You may sling the mask on a branch
when questions fail, nothing's been procured
to flatten the curve. States scramble for gowns
and ventilators the breath will stain. Keep your keep
your distance to be watched always without a sunset clause.
Anything alone acted is an accident shared
whatever the fear, with skin hunger
pushing *con* to *tang* in refute.
What's app what's app what's appened, who
were you next to, just a pair of lacy knickers
jutting from a split bin bag. It's no use blaming
a phone mast for the ooze that clings
but whatever it takes is a tall promise to meet
as week by week the bills come in.

If a tiger gets it, he doesn't take one for the team,
no, his Hello stutters and trips from hill to hell
messing fire between stripes—fierce electric
quivers unable to spring. We're all in the zoo or quad:
stirring a quarantini with a biro
to sip before dinner
won't pharma these frights away.

———

A farmer might favour these grass-sprung streets
hearing long after breakfast a chiffchaff's name
pump branches under a blue sky. The jet trails have gone
though the odd spiv will race, tense under lockdown.
A beast lurks in the background
ready to take from fever another message
as by a stir of air Death's grasp opens
to let us dance again. Milder to Moulder might ask
how'd you hold force in terror, with experts shunned
to bleach the lungs. Follow the science, says our deputy
when some say, others say Alone with the Alone
won't catch it, kill it, bin it. Rooms hung with jasper and gold
lie deserted while bodies cluster in a poke of receding space
with dungeon light. What's home where nothing fits
like apron curls and slipped goggles? You breathe
and breed, you touch and take on or dispatch—it's dirt
made by the system that has to come back
pushed at an angle, forgotten in a bardo folly. I'm not you
as our faces merge, the thing burns out to a blank.
This closed chamber has no windows or doors, and scarier
it has no ceiling or walls. I'm a floating whiteness,
you can't have more story, but there's charcoal smoking

in my brain. A lottery screen says move freely
while the frame is a zombie cartoon, the mime version
collapsing intent. Jerks nip the arrested
in a fine spring, not flowers or birds but us, stuck on alert.
As I doomscroll through the latest, with a shut globe
and marked boards reading the wound
I find myself in a tree house or water tower
leafed and gushing, then abroad in a spacious field
by a hilltop flushed in the morning sun. A man
with long silver hair squeezes a word to fruit, he is Milton
in Lancelot's wake trusting in a crown laid up—
the lot cast in the lap for those who finish well.
Will this wash blots from a blazing skull
and spongy passage, get limbs all a tremble to climb
any crag and trace the way back to an easy quilt?

Logodaedale
to Ovid in Tomis

All right, I'm not banished to a wind-torn coast
beyond, with harsh-tongued riders roughly dressed
bearing down. There's no spear to pierce
my breast or freezing air to squeeze my throat,
the water doesn't coil in rage as mythical monsters
twist my shape, the stars—come from nowhere—
don't make a hostile map. Wine still flows from bottles
I laid in store, a friend fetches asparagus
and salmon, with the bag of nuts I crave. I wander
in a garden I know, hot enough for Rome.

I don't have to tell this book to shun any fellow
as a song that kills. But here on this soil,
clamped by the prime bully who wields a bolt
fearful of germs that pass unseen,
I could be in exile. Days, nights bleed into each other
and words will only travel as a distant roll:
can't you hear me, S.O.S. I despair at lagging lines
which tread unmusical like rust of older speech,
you said it forever on that black limit
where in a paler zone I merely dip and spill.

The work may hold long after Jupiter crumbles
reversing badges of blame and fame.
Shaggy pages, blots, carry the stress of loss
in recovered story, which is a sort
of armed hand. You frame words in silence
pulled by the sea's icy grip, one channel coursing
beneath another—salt against fresh.

On the fever-plain verses will sometimes run
in a stretch of smarts, poised in the void
to reach a reflector out there who thinks remote.

I dream I'm in the garden where my lover goes
to bathe by violets and jasmine. Her song will spread life
through statues, her scent will drive sickness
from the air, her kiss will ripple to the heart's core.
Were there hell to pay and the scene slip
to a moss-grown shed or a court with a cloud of dust
accusing the oldest art, those lets would premise
some lasting spirit. I hold my ear close
and wait for the link that proves we are bodied,
juice in fibre at the delta of found sense.

Our long steel rail has no rasping vowels
and the sky isn't cracked by traffic,
it's just the count at a clipped remove stains this peace
where we cannot press lips or grasp any hand.
Starlings swoop and rise in a thickening swarm
that curves, cancels and zigzags, a dot-cohort
keeping neighbour-close to range an uncertain field.
Figures came from Lombardy but someone thought it
better to wait, a snout guarding the herd. Would a ghost
care to know how the Thames flows after the Po?

Wherever you lie, most likely outside the gates
in a vault lit by stone lamps—strangely constant—
lend us your nerve to face this plague
where harsh or kind it seems that the world
has one nose. I sail and walk with you in a tower
deeply dug, where one tongue glows

over a purple tunic. Bronzed in the shadow-flame
you are hardly a wizened mummy and I didn't enter
by a code of knocks. Maybe we'll toggle between states
to outwit the patrol and bring laughter back.

Shell-case

He can't get into the house. Who?…
You know where you are, don't you?
Yes, in the film.
We've been taking care of you for a long time.
You can't see anyone.
Why is that that? I'm sleeping.
I want to see.
Do you want me to pop that leg back up?
We don't have any jogging bottoms
Where are you?
I want to go to Charing Cross.
You're already at Charing Cross.
Have you seen anything else other than these sheets?
They're all dandelions. Is it my slippers?
Can you see my hand? Which one's moving now?
Which one? Nothing-a-tore.
Whose turn is it? All out, all out.
Number two is wantum if Tuesday will let me.
I got there before didn't I? Can you talk between the pips?
It's like Arabic. What happens if you owe them money?
We'll just draw the curtains.
Did you bring me a sandwich—it's dancing,
I've been asleep all day.
No, you've been talking quite a bit.
Help, help. You've got to get us out—anyway
that's why I called the doctor.
I've got to sit up, I want to sit up, I want to get out.
How can I when you're all around me
telling me to do things.
I'm not stupid. My brain Is a pomegranate

cut In half or it's my heart beating.
Mum, mum … I need to speak to me mother.
You're not going to get the rest of it.

November 1918

The war done, another rages, here
as if in somebody else's skin.
Not ghostly green or any colour
across the field
it enters to fill and split: lungs, ribs, throat.
There is wrath between selves, nations
but this flies indiscriminate. On an ordinary day
a walker drops to the pavement or a rider
topples from a horse.

And who'll notice
when a foe comes silent and sightless
through the air?

In a rented house on Stephen's Green
the spirit refuses questions
while the great clock in the hall is stopped.
Georgie, now known as George
and six months' pregnant, tosses and turns upstairs,
gasping for breath. Her form hovers
between states as Maud—owner on the doorstep—
is turned away
lest a tracker raise a second angry wind.

Freed from Holloway, disguised as a Red Cross nurse
and without a passport, 'Moura' has crossed the sea
to get home. What's possession
in a building or the head, says he
caught between you's in a line of trouble.
She's the countess in a violet cloak with silver clasp

dragging on a last cigarette
and she's the voice of the crowd, shrill and bitter
shrugging off the oppressor.
There's more to do than sit and sew, sifting sheets
when everything is remembered.

One will accuse the other, as a pet hare
munches grass and leaves in the garden
and a tag records a pippin
grown onto rootstock with luminous skin.
A moody sky threatens to force the branches back
and drench the path leading down.

Beyond the railings a barrel organ cranks its tune
over again and a tram-car swerves and hisses
to a halt. Clang and throb before that
of swans and ducks. A sheath of air spirals
from the lake: figures lean away
as hands join. What we did is always
with us, a stain of beauty in common cloth
and no third person can judge. You may think to go
unseen in a covert with bird notes attuned
to your song, but from paths open to all
a dog's fangs will nose you out.

The water is a tin flash, the bridge is a grooved bone,
the drowned poem stares up.

Laughing atoms show we're not made up
of what was claimed, the latest news must give.
A black town is sometimes red in the dusk
and the deuce take any rule forbids
this eviction staged as a lantern show.

Two years since a potshot through a club window
and some kindness from one ready to kill.

A square captured leads to the same
in riposte, as prisoners trudge
beneath a four-corner sky. Your field of fire
is a groined ceiling, laid in style
across the river, a shout with an endless pause
by polished stone. Is this just
the bagman's folly, doing Alexander again
in a slimy trench? To go willy-nilly
from one hole to another
getting a yard where you wanted a mile
and acting false to break out truth.

If that's a script of uncertain credit
it's not all fireworks
when a country treads on another's behind.

This makes a plot roll
in blocks of sevens, each dot
the call to another life. She who shuddered
at soldiers gored by the war bull
would now run rifles through gorse. She who charts
the course of things from centuries back
must shut out the irrelevant. Lungs and funnels
dictate in a castle cell or warmer bedroom.

When you think it's past, it starts again:
a bursting head, aching legs, a fire of cold shivers.
He can't throw his arms around her but must
move to a room in the club. A brass plate
won't announce as white blood cells churn.

Across town a dancer falls to the boards
stiff, coffins are stacked 18-high, streets are sprayed
with Jeyes fluid.

Flipped, exhausted, the patient sits up
in a shawl and blanket to pick at fish and cream
got with a doctor's permit. Somehow after the end
there's relief—and sleep without drugs—
though all's unfair in the year of can't even.

Afraid of a stranger, afraid of a friend,
 you hardly trust yourself.
This window is a jackal's eye
piercing private space, this chimney is a chute
dropping soot in the bed.
A gentle hand touching your shoulder
won't erase the corolla that flashed from your skull.
In a crimp of time, past a row of houses
one on a coal black horse twists
to show his ashen face
as by an arch
his accomplice whispers a metallic song.

Wrongly called, our Spanish Lady
has the odds and evens of it,
twenty to nothing and nineteen to one—
she'll dance you down a corridor,
whirl through any door.
In a marble entrance and then under rickety stairs
she'll claim a kiss, she's got so much to share.

Lurching in grooves to get to another place
there's little to put you safe, the sequel winds
through episodes that promise a close
and just wander, a loss in each sense of Z.

All the Helens that go projected
in a voltascope
won't make this mate disappear, she stares
and holds a candle
that might be a fiddle or guitar by the bone-fire.
Maybe this mends our errors, maybe
it's a silk veil, but the floating form pushes one year
into the next and we move on.

A poet dips in the tub to know, finds a coil of figures
to shape vision, and still at the nub
has to deal with I-come you-go germs, the splodges
in cream sheets that live to fill a book.

Out-pass

You want to be with them and the way is barred
or they're in another land, across latchets or brackish water

not a friend or relation to touch, will we again
share thoughts in the moment

church and school empty, finger of the clock stuck

but still the bodies come
elbowing past in grass that's gone to mud

they're us and they're not, solo-intent in massed ranks

I think it's a dog squeaks and gibbers
squirming in fungal white

as here an insect crawls from breeding wood cells

we're in a field contracted
to the floor of a shack

and step between clammy ghosts
with decomposing ankles

* * * * *

The cure isn't just an itchy fix
whatever the table urges

like 'virus removal' by neon flashes

we're clad or sealed off with perjured fingers
body and tower in a spool of words

apocka-cocker-lipsy

is this villanous or villainous and does it matter
for a frog breather

a mask with jerking feet

what do I do, what do I want glazed by a code
in a spilling tray of devices

the more you have the more you want, glittering
back in dust

an air purifier whisper-quiet or ranunculus spread

with no marvel heave
as yesterday speaks with sweat

* * * * *

A child drags a sheet along the empty road
and it swirls in your face

who's worth saving, that other
in the image of our own

a wrinkled lizard on a stretcher

sausage figures
huddled round the firepit

or a window imp
who'd like to swing on a rope

you flip through proofs for the word mis-set

which slated for a box of pills
could be boner or bonus

you dream of poppies in a bowl
as the room is adopted by a stiff smock

and then you bite on stone

* * * * *

One demon fended off,
another creeps in and glides forward

'introduce me good fellow'

mimic sweetness in stale breath
that clings

'a double portion will fizz in keen iambics'

I squint at bird stains on a blurry trolley
and see nothing's future-proof

'why then, just here you'll break the wall'

stuck on repeat we press the plastic
and chomp, aching for a buzz

as weirdly the seasons turn into one
with distant stuff come home

zinctum zanctum, it's a bad place

if in this passage we're our own gods
and the record won't tally, what then?

Silent Inferno

Through a bird mask what runs sweet
over the bridge
comes to taste metallic

tell me grafter, would you lick that dragonzello
you gave someone else, bulging yellow or hectic red

a guy like you can walk through any speech backwards—
it's just a molestation in the pit
before the real junket

when/done/load/before/each/cell
to test if it rages

the swabs will make a catch

       * * * * *

But why play the geometer and rummage
to nail a demon
making tears in squinted eyes

this scheme could be a skit, bobbing slowly on silver

whose fault can be pinned
in flashes
magnate to beggar
with babble from each gaping throat

are you nobody, hiding with the contracts out

ledger on ledge, coin in casino boat, proctor by spangles
darn me I can't tell, here in pale blue smoke

a thousand forms I didn't file or assign

* * * * *

At the funnel base all denominations mix
in red-hot rock or ice

no helicopters blink signals, no sirens whine

just a fragment of fear remains
as every package left at the door

starts to gurgle

oh Fontella, this wickerwork of nerves
is like a twig bleeding

she so far-off, mmm-hmm, mmm-hmm
voice like a fooork in nevery balba
aching charms

elsewheretic (the message floats)

* * * * *

Hello from the inside, I'm pressed to the wall
an almond-eyed mosaic
unreachable

did we dance, yes, no—maybe

in a touch passing kin you'd lift me
thigh to head as a waterspout

gypsy swung, volgarizzamento
a shimmer of flesh
sprung from lines dropped on the library floor

you see, breath itself entraps

choked in a side chamber
they judge us who don't harm

tracing our fate in a twisted spill
when really we glide, wrapped in a snow-flame cocoon

      * * * * *

Follow the evidence to keep from losing
your smell and taste

who ever listens to conjurers—we're not
picking each other's scabs like the scales of a bream,
we're not stretched on a slab in an underground corridor

Mr or Mrs God in chemtrail verse
is trying to set you right with a rhubarby stick

come-close, go-away, clap and sack

a glass of wine is the brim of the whole world,
only then can you wring consent

* * * * *

Goldenmouth's grease yields to a cluster of cases
that can't be concealed

his eleven-mile pouch is one ghostly theremin,
a foreboding of what is known—
the dead lining up to mosey and zigzag
with not a saint to swear by

in another take it's a forest of lampposts with hanging bulbs

a club under the railway arch
will let you dance if you get a wristband
rave-tranced with a fog machine

uniform is king behind a padlocked door

you'll wear a trench in the ground
swirling—what was first, the noun or the verb
moiling why others should do it—
steal a kiss with numb lips

if the shutters are down
do we have to fuck with our coats on

never, ever, no never, no

* * * * *

Leaders squeeze chums through any defile,
their swish of gold turning to a trudge of lead

just a misdemeanour will lift you to the other house
and no printer will print it

if one partied hard telling people to keep apart,
if one chose wallpaper with a favour wiped,
if one crossed borders telling people to stay put

could they say
what a tree means or a pool
inscribed in biro with a coffee stain
under a cloud of banknotes

start-up saviours for a sausage roll or a punk pint
have absent fingers to build the rescue model

                    * * * * *

Can you read the way as your face melts

plodding with a guide to the last bound, or maybe
the closest

there to finger a lancet in grey rock
and climb through

(I strive to make blighted speech work again)

is this what we knew when it wasn't an act
and things just existed

a chain of gold threaded through the air,
streets and stairs peaking in a parade of planets
which fire livelier than a devil or middle spirit's show

now we soul-search the dawn
remembering how each watch changes

a scar in a lilac leaf, almost whole

as in nitrate gaps
the credits roll

Love in Epidemia

Head punctured by an amoeba, pulse
of feet crawling

        in a slow corridor

                your nerve-spirit

a stain of light in an organ pipe

           has a diver's breath

     hair glued on a crust

             twisting tendrils

splodge of a mouth, wax off alabaster

               let me recite

        abracadabra   strings of syllables

to get to the window frame

       and prise its bars

x-ray stark

      my matchsticks march

             as lever-words

    accidentallow

a figure   to slip from a shining net

  even here   privily joined

out of place you broke on me my wave

Knottyrotica

The hand in the margin says
        this is a radiant passage,
mingled ores to taste
        in the first letter
catching the lady's smile

She could be sprung from the sea
        with seed pearls in red velvet
a presence to stroke and kiss
        a scent from a wanderlust candle
like cups of drowse for a dream tale

eau de cologne and rose-water
        slightly brackish
you rub you wear
        in a flick or flip
reading the fondest flash

Here in Duke Humfrey's Library
        sunlight falls in still air
with a whiff of pencil shavings
        and rich tea biscuits
pointing to the essence you hold

a folded sliding block will make a handle to hear
        one ception on all the others
the stone stony, the moss greenly felted
        the thrushes songly feathered
a picture bodied in a word gone through

sprawl as vital departure
       to know what is
the thing we're in
       cloven to join in a loop
that returns—the part about which fits

2. A Cricklewood Sequence

1. Kossoff's Garden

A field in a house,
derelict boards in the corner,
a dialogue with cast-offs
under paint-sodden newsprint

not a story but threads
of day to day trial

second burden of a child's window-gaze

a diesel train
races through pear and cherry trees,
one limb propped
on a wooden stake

memory grid between stops
tangy, grubby
in springing passage

the rails open a landscape
pulse across scrub

round upon round of states
yellow on blue, grease streaks
a fix on a swerve

ghost orchard before redbrick house
beaten, chopped
to get there from nothing

2. Cellular Scan

What trace of those taken away
(door-seal words)

     breath remains in walked-up
     stigmas

magnolia in Mapes wood
halo

       I-ed other vestige

   to not deflect

the points

    flutely thrown

heel to halfclock   here struck
lastly   alive

second light from a green vein

     against   tar march scores

either's maul or smother

3. Devonian Exile

Does here live Erich? Ah yes,
here we are staying

I am the last nobody
in our revolution

    (a vow to disappoint)

Be anxious of those without doubt,
must always listen

a pocket of bone-dust

    to collect hope
    from solvable matter

like the contents
of every bin for a mile around

    lost objects impel
    another muster
    to shape a language

a tin can, a piece of lace, a knife
always a little outside

4. Morgan Studios

Footprint of names
on highroad corner, now a Saver wedge

    control room high in cloud
    over bass rumble

haunting coat of organ

To feel tomorrow like you feel today,
    repeat and fade

    dead room for drums
    (subtle kink)

      A single piano note,
    submarine ping,
    return of son of nothing
through Mistress Leslie's horn

    Robot whirr and whoosh
    (someday
      they'll understand)

      Gyroscope
  a fleet dance   of keys
    over bass walk
    and time that isn't

Eyelid film
split city, lonely at the bar
under green wall
blue-black beats
to what she says
while kids howl

5. Hellraiser: St Gabriel's Road

The right to be an uncommon man
offstage he's always on

Head down to the Salisbury, wake up in Mexico
blue eyes across a desert

not remarking light or weather,
just the smoke
from room to room

They're all gone, why am I still here?

Sydney jumps into the open coffin,
sits on his master's chest as people sigh
farewell

a cat, rolling upon prank
knows there's never a master

    (what's new) cherub or tiger

Bless the cork that bounces,
the cross you leap from
to perform a dance

toes, teeth, ears put to the test

    outside watching
    yourself
    watching yourself

star-gable over ox-eye daisies and sorrel

Dying is easy, comedy is hard

6. Ivy Den

Turfed out with a jester's record, earnest
like a bluebottle round the light

    tried to trot through space
    for the common dole

one long programme in a microscope
failing the radio probe

citizen with nasal drawl, *n'yeah sure*
promises … not a miracle

    the base fare
    a smirk in plotting

to stop floods, fumes

    or is the contract misverted
    for sky-pods and bendy carriers

Of the past we make a future

    salamander, down a piece
    from the water tower

beard of leaves twisting copper
to the upper storey
a mask for all behind

self planted as a silver birch,
grapes, olives by a large pond

lines eclectic to quote   as critics hover
you must take the odd chance
between pious and fry us—
what doesn't kill makes strong

Notes to the Cricklewood Sequence:

1: Leon Kossoff. Chatsworth Road.
2: Paul Celan. Willesden Lane ('Tarranbrae')/Mapesbury Road.
3: Erich Fried. Dartmouth Road.
4: 169-71 Willesden High Road. The Kinks, various from *Lola Versus Powerman* through to *Preservation Act 1*; Pink Floyd, 'Echoes'; Fairport Convention, 'Mr Lacey'; Gordon Beck, *Gyroscope*; Lou Reed, *Berlin*.
5: Peter O'Toole.
6: Ken Livingstone. Ivy Road.

3.

Political Poems
&
Tribute Poems

Limen

The Jack of trumps will lead you in, a scarlet coat with gold crowns. Suckled on gunpowder. A town within itself, with streets, yards, green behind massive walls and chimneys. Rumble of traffic muffled, mournful hoot and echoes from the river. Smoky vapour, something between mist and fog. Masked angles, storeys—elsewhere, elsewhen otherwise. This gateway built and rebuilt, strong in quaking earth.

White keep, mortar tempered by the blood of beasts. Space to protect or enforce, display or confine. Place of departed bodies and those who still attend. Family closet with mottoes, verses, hieroglyphics. Trial of honour as a turning word. Repeated stairs and corridors.

A house for the shearing of gold (bar to disc). In another, at the top, an unspeakable number of arrows. Next a curve with wooden houses, latticed: three lionesses, one lion of great size, a tiger, a lynx, a lean, ugly wolf, a porcupine and an eagle. An elephant, with which the Lord Treasurer is little in love, given wine in winter to keep out cold. An avenue of trees, a portcullis like an open jaw. Passage and stairs to a lord's sleeping-kennel. Court to a tower new fronted. The jewel-room: steps down to a small cell in the thickness of the wall, its vaulted, groined roof just visible.

A pageant of motley. Halberdiers in line. The block, with hollow for a duke's head. Solid oak. A throng that gapes for novelty. Those who watch think a pardon has been brought, with thunder or the earth rumbling. Some are squeezed into the moat. It is just a rider in haste. Eyes like slit grapes. Would you wrestle with the Scavenger's daughter, span reduced within hoops? Bleed from every orifice, a course meet for this cause.

What name is on the warrant? Are you sure it's me you want? Neither any one of which.

It is worth a laugh, a song or two with barrels of ale. Moon aspects only, all performance. Are the locks, chains, bolts and bars in good order? This ruff is too high, and the sword should hang—thus. Up and down to search, every chink that holds a mouse. Open then shut: that distant and measured respect which authority pays as a tax to decorum.

Incomparable gleam behind glass and steel. A crown encrusted with jewels, impossible to hold. But cut the cable and that system of wires will be old rope. Your master craftsman will make his way, given the perfect instant.

One word and a head rolls. Some are stretched, others walk openly, marking a stone for every turn they take. A show of Bethlehem, a labour of translation. Orange juice for secret correspondence. A hen-roost for tubes and retorts. A generating cell for conjecture after wider room is denied.

Your childhood's dreadful nursery, a combination of reels. Here again you would not be counterfeit. With a pocket blade as wand of office, loosen the stone around the bolt, squeeze through and up to the roof. Fling an iron ball with rope to the outer wall and slide down. Pray you are not watched. Row a pretty mile, partner with fortune, then wipe this smeared constellation.

Pretends ignorance but confesses in substance.

Can say no more but 'nay', without I should open my body. I am cruelly handled as was never seen, but I think the King does it to prove me [laughs]. If any man accuse, I can say but 'nay', and they can bring no witnesses.... Where is my sweet brother? … Never a prince had wife more loyal in all duty and true affection. Let not any light fancy or bad counsel withdraw your favour from me.

Pallets? They might make ballads well now. One blow of a sharp bastard sword. A rocket rises. Betrothal again tomorrow.

The voice of the land speaks in my tongue. The true legitimate. A confused tallying, as treason's innocence. She hangs her head like poppies heavy with rain. A dream of empire that briefly danced. No gazers admitted, to wet their handkerchiefs and report how like a saint she ended.

Either two makes a play, spelled spacious. Five hundred friends and now not one, a pile of Troy hollow weights. Should they be even that.

Guns for the Queen's birthday, bonfires to be made in every street.

A room of strict seclusion, no news exchanged. Guards on parade, drill sharp as any in Prussia. Bagpipes.

Whisper of a failed rising. Pull a bent nail out of the wall and swallow it. Then a tiny flask of curare from your jacket tail. Choke and slobber. Warm coat taken away. Clothes, worn for month, slimy still from the inlet. Two soldiers in the cell, another looking in. Three men with eyes never averted, night and day, changed every hour, and the single bulb always full on. Sleep impossible. Thought a page of Hell.

Durance. Endure. Duress. You dream to find a porter carrying many keys. Throw him to the ground, unlock the door, let every inmate out to loose others' bonds.

Roar of flames, hissing of water pipes, crowbars at the portal. Orbs, diadems and sceptres borne through fiery midnight, leaving fused metal with bayonet-points bristling like long blades of grass.

All obstacles must be removed. Brother, another's mistress, nephews. Is not the world a big butt of humour, into which we'll put a duke? Sweet liquid in which to tumble. She comes back, always will. Winds whirl and the walls buckle. Is wine replacing blood in your veins? The people wish to see their king. But his diamond sceptre squeaks (found and cut in a later century). Laughing voices greet him.

And this is proof of the theory that the London cockney—that is to say, the real costermonger, with his dark eyes and head like Julius Caesar and his wife with flashing teeth, raven locks and a love of bright colours—is actually a descendant of the Romans who built the Tower of London.

A head buried in the White Mount, so no plague shall ever come across the sea. *Bran vras*: raven. Lost voice digging a new passage in shifts. Clods of earth cast forth. Freedom we died for you. Sea of poppies in a green ditch.

Who comes here? The Keys. Whose keys? No such message, no such home. If in my journey *out*, if I forbore, if it were lawful, if it was *they*, if I might elsewhere have … all this I have done because. Others persuade my silence but I intend and have hewn out further volumes. Sun reverberates on the ledge. My name has never been my own but belongs to the Authorities, who forbid me to change or withhold it, as a ring on the collar of a beast.

Orbital diagrams to conjugate infinity. Must answer to shapes in your dream, spotted or swampy, spinning to solid crystal.

Whisper into tape these wards are weak, there's better lodging on the moon. A burn cup to angels' eyes. But summons to summons brings something back, alien shocks inside. Your has been or future fold makes certain now: they have used stasis cubes to enter three-dimensional paintings in the gallery.

I could bring down your government with one word ... Well, not a single word, just six. Dazzled eyes take no view.

Under the blue light they turn on their heel and begin to march from the room, as though hypnotised.

Sycorax have got hold of a vial of A Positive. We may be caught in an aggregate of last moments: wicket open and Troy turned to ashes.

Would you be too historical? What (a)vails truth? A stack of discs to rearrange. Red, blue, yellow, green, brown. Target arousal. Clips to pair under theme. Or is this numb noting: oil in obligation, on the same page or from Mars. Not an easy site to get around. Just another word for a house you can't get out of. If people don't know what to call it, it goes unrecorded.

They misreport the tale or else I cannot speak English.

Sources:

Ainsworth, *The Tower of London*; Susan Brigden, *Thomas Wyatt: The Heart's Forest*; John Dickson Carr, *The Mat Hatter Mystery*; Charles Cestre, *John Thelwall*; Corman (dir.), *The Tower of London*; *Cruikshank's Omnibus*; Dekker and Webster, *The Famous History of*

Sir Thomas Wyatt; *Doctor Who*, episodes 167 and 240; Ford Madox Ford, *The March of History*; W.S. Gilbert, *The Yeomen of the Guard*; Edward Hall, *Chronicle*; Hawthorne, *The English Notebooks*; Paul Hentzner, *Travels in England*; Christobel Hood, *The Book of Robert Southwell*; Brian Inglis, *Roger Casement*; David Irving, *Hess: The Missing Years*; Eric Ives, *The Life and Death of Anne Boleyn*; Gerald Kersh, 'Karmesin and the Crown Jewels'; *The Mabinogion*, second branch; Malory, *Le Morte d'Arthur*; John Morris, *The Life of Father John Gerald*; Matthew Paris, *English History 1235-73*; PEBL blog: 'Tower of London Test'; Pepys, *Diary*; Pynchon, *Mason & Dixon*; Sir Walter Ralegh, *The History of the World, Letters*; Rowe, *Lady Jane Grey*; Scott, *The Fortunes of Nigel*; Mary Shelley, *The Fortunes of Perkin Warbeck*; Sterne, *A Sentimental Journey*; Stowe, *Annals*.

Quo Warrento

Of A[mb]er's hasty blush...
Winters of Memory seemed to roll
       —Byron, *The Giaour*

Who deserves, is part of our dream   she smiles
to the faithful

              beaming home
              the moans

to hero-butt remoaners   over beer or tea

            an echo of rump belief

pure in farragoland   (come out of money)

See through compound drams
the swamp beneath sheen, a steaming vapour

         ***

Of what constitutes your force

        that glittering neck with snaky heads s

            lashed
                to draw power

a viscid tip
for wondrous feats

we must get the lowdown

figures we
[emend] *privately*
may see

to toughen the test

***

Unbind ourselves from meddlesome rules
traitors use for benefit

noses poked   with sense interlined

from foreign shelves

debris dragged

a-throb   into easy quarters   a native couldn't

access   (features, future set)

where sniffs of nappy juices

tell of a deeper drench

***

We must execute laws to stop pestilent traffic

and not be swayed

by grumbletonians

cradled into thinking high

    at the mantly-chimney

while wetherspoons are poxed

      in a learner's box

no state's conscience will allow

      ***

Cling/fling   the pieces we would save

    an ideal market

ready for stop or go

    (not my) green fracked
      in truth transhistorical

Plug and seal another tier

    of what we're meant to wipe

(ruin of manufacture … maybe a waste inquiry?)

      ***

Armoured with thermal dust you fight

     for the core

a last stand on Scenleag ridge

       to keep off otherwise kin

not wavering, shrinking   from wedge or breastwork

Rallied by a vote   you can restage anything

a querked tapestry would argue

      biodetail
       as
      neutron
      sallies

if we can cultivate stars   each for itself

       by
      brick-shit
      licence

this body-drama   updates the secret

a premier plate blue model

     ***

I give you a certain hungry wish

      the thing you'd rather

           not admit

the nasty parade   done to ravish

        ***

Beast hook over lapping serfs

      (proud in the trough)

whose bile will authorize   removal

(home/self in slices)   an interest

a con in the jokescape   takes

        advantage

the same order   whatever

      the guard

might be a pot to boil

        ***

The plot discovered   voice of tens of thousands

in a chatroom frame   convenient to blast

      character

         the humble picker or student

     a threat to all

       poses

(did I hear right   across the void)

     ***

Rude reflection: you prove

     the disease

       by producing

         the remedy

words locked   to ensure   what plays into
hope

    How to keep the lights on

      get fish fingers and crisps

when   *too many*   want a bite

the argot won't
    transmit

not by gage or writ

    in a hooded moment

    ***

Liberty walks with a gag in her mouth

under some cosmic gape   while reckonably

this whole ground   will cry

let's spin out of zone control

Marks outside the Spa

i.m. Chris Torrance

A woman with a baby between her legs
covered with red ochre—
anointment deep in forest shade

where a meteor might have crashed,
mildew on emulsion

Two roe deer antlers point up
from her head
a furry helmet with teeth dangling over eyes

as if she were the landscape

Curved bones frame her face
leaving the mouth open to chant or scream

Below the neck
a necklace—bones and teeth of a bison or boar—
stretches

It can't be graphed, it stares out from what
travelled between worlds

the animal mother
dismembered and put back whole
through sweat and herbs

Numbness, itching, to get secrets
from an ancestor

the gift in shock

To faint, to see double, to throw limbs
and vent noises in foam

To control weather, tell the future and heal the sick
acting the like over power disordered

a mottled zone, a body pummelled in bloody surf

Not your fairy-story heroine
with stolen shoes and stockings
but after afraid in rings of smoke

A pit dancer with locked syllables, the current
between roots
nameless in foretime

yields a veiny sack-print,
threads of feeling, ferns and fungi in the outer air

All our share in now, swaddling to release
by jolted breath what lurked in loam—
a dare or forced need

still a hoard in hoary holt, if carried from base
for show within glass

The drummelled parkland waits
velvet between nipple and navel,
keeps an echo in children's cries

blazing with posthumous light
yes, o yes, o yes—longways as many as will

Line of What Make or Sort

for J.H. Prynne

Here is the mouthway through spirit-walls
set transverse like baffle-plates. A blind tread
by studded doors to a green court.

Bleak-sheen, shards and grains
with a smooth face. Widewhere story
brought to a point, up a spiral
that becomes a candle halo.

In a case of doughty slips you work
from word to idea.

              That disherited
brings weighty strokes from wandering—
burden of the utmost isle in drifty sea.

Water-cords fall on the glass, as inside
a planting pocket asks what throw of terms
will make the leaf in white halves
stand mobile.

             A stretch of free air
closed at the corner, troysome, for those
searching an elixir greatly animal, full of metal.

Memories of hall-joy on island gravel
(no marvel against kind) dart from contemplation
as a spark from burning coals.

This *paradosis* comes over stone to the exit
window, where all is re-verded
to address *trayfoyles and trewloves*
but dispel the mark that ties.

                        For who knocks
a poet is everywhere, nowhere and abroad—
the blanks attest that longer watch.

Fifth from the ground
a book with a register half crossed out
will open the place you sometimes walk.

Orange skies, Mr Lee, Mr Lee
over the flatland

                        a windmill stark by waving reeds

            small boat in sluggish water

        spearshaft tree at the sedge-side,
        keys about to scatter

the aura to speak, centuries in sun-sight
ravelled

                    deal

                        new terms

        (the yen
        to go
        waist deep)

we took they took the gift that is rice paste
over rivets

        can offer to power
           a bulbous steam ball
        with rods flashing

a temple over crushed mulberries

      sinolacquer   turbine switch

a bird finger theory of need

             O missed fellow
             that should be here

    fathom and nail

this humbug strake

          or lightly deflect the barrage

(spring tune to bitter lyric)

Arthur's sword shines on a blazer pocket, his giant
comes a marvel from the east.

No risk assessment for a glowing soul, got to
step right in, what hood is smoking black.

Any tulk you take will say his tub
is crammed with florins, for which read debt record
on a ferris wheel screaming Jesus.

The story has heads unfair, with matted locks
that ask for chicken wages,
a transaction apart the media shower.

But it's too late, as the other said, to drop back
to the straight-on plot, we go like a verb
through sense.

                    Can't unring the bell or be rid
of ventures. Across space you cleave and clutch
to sideling stir.

                    Expression comes as we move
in a crinkled passage with each twitch of a silk cord.
By serial wonder it shapes a tale outside
the bound state, gut syllabic.

Acutest self at compass edge, jade under blur of cloud.

Early Marks

I first heard you on paper, a Fulcrum ghost
in Parker's on the Broad

    nobody attended and I took an hour packed
    to move through the lines
    fluid in take

        a little face
        distant
        at the long jubilee table

    bunting hung out

as the king calls 'be a useful citizen'

I was the learning hand, like you somehow left
with smiles and the odd glare
in grainy toyland

    but the longhair climate gave means
    to feel oblique

        the things how they come
        a gash in brick
        a stream beneath

    local-placed and sliding in different nows

a film or canvas foreign with jump cuts

At Warwick eleven years on your voice alive
brought that obligation to bear

     in 'most of an unpublished and could be
     as-yet-unwritten poem'

          a score for objects
          less of a game
          in the prism

     it was a chart to put my footprint
     back in

gold remembered in a stain of porcelain

A few months later, upstairs at The Three Horseshoes
after a riot of I Can't Give You Anything But Love
finding corners through the obvious
beneath Nuttall's cornet

     you had the audience in fits
     reporting your engagement and missed contact
     with Avis Tree, researcher

          text spun to identity theft

     while inside the laugh was a struggle

     to reach exactly across the gap

Silent Glabber

i.m. Glen Cavaliero

The carpet of moss on this bank seems to ask
will you listen
to the throb that lies beneath

it's a familiar flank, the boughs overhead
whispering give us your ink-blood

emerald in black the gasp of what's held down
makes a rustle-hum
rippling at the rim of mind

a don who leafs the pages has its spirit
in his shoulder blades

bone and tissue to brain
footstep in sky—
notes etched from the understorey

Strata

for Geraldine Monk

I

Steers is the stage you land   beneath the ridge
and between two nabs   one cut like a knife

scar-wake words   in a cleft   or ledge
to pull and scramble

tightly wound shells   a ribbed curl
or something vanished   with astro-claws

blue-hearted rock   beneath yellow

it is not easy   it is not

the yield for folk who know   fire and ice traces

lead to light   like an outlaw prism

a beck in the glen   sides downthrowing

a memory pulse

2

Scetune at Domesday   in mizzle
where mermaids were gaoled   and fled   with a curse

cottages squeezed South   facing wind-arrows
from the North

red tiles shake   over bonnets and granzies

herring, cod and turbot   (when did you last…?)
fished from sharp bows or square stern

if the catch   over months   is bad
kill a pigeon, remove its heart   stick it full of pins
and burn   over a charcoal fire

3

Cook, the boy, handles cloth   but the yarn he wants
is all of whales   sliding beneath   the ocean's skin

clicks, buzzes, squeaks   a song in deep sleepscape

his course   to sound and mark   straits, islands, strands
through shrill cries   heavy squalls
a cask lashed   with stuff to keep health

by telescope and plumb   to answer mindcraves
then warping nearer the shore
in the skirts of a wood   to find   the naked native

who is the wiser   and placed elemental
rank reversed   as you turn a grocer's list

bread fruit   xxxxxx   salt mud creatures

4

a call   unexpected
at high tide   the bowsprit of a coble
sprung   through   the window
of the Cob and Lobster

something more than a pint
or a pipe of tobacco

fierce in the flood

5

      a fish skin purse
packed with   SILVER   coin
     run   or rolled for
by a man or boy   in a sack

festival sports   in a war year
when you might   be pressed

6

jet earrings   on the dinosaur coast   glistening night

a small sign that ties   a world to a body

suspended

as gulls screech   *ah-wa-a-ah*

do they say owt   by step, fret and key

over ruby dulse   a taste of anchovy or Marmite

7

no need to scribble a formula   up high
as a chained task   unless it's a spell   to summon spirits
or ward off   bone-break   or soul-peck

town lass   by a circle   of tawny grisettes
and a rotting log

then at head level   a cowl clinging to a trunk
phosphorescent orange

you tread back   like the lost crew

through peaty runnels   and salt-bitten grass
to doorway   and hearth

where the pages come   thrawn and (com)pounded

or lightly drawn   a whole tone

soundseared   through the scratch of a needle
tick-tick waves   in string xxxxx
to spark pictures

spores   lifetalk in deathtalk

a face picked out   by a candle

S & G Variations
for Jeff Hilson

Just a little pipe organ charts newfound earth
swirling the moon on an open field

      she reads the last issue careless with intent,
      you in the note, the note in you

a dream on a plane and a bus
filtered through glass

      is it *l'amour* or *la mort*, come to look for
      the starting clinch

don't know how we made it, those road cobbles
a silver stream

      two countries to address
      everly pitched

kew-eek in a zigzag
jug-jug on a thorny branch

      could make one perfect person, each fit
      over and coming in

but celluloid against flesh
is a taller deal behind one cut short

      the hair curls different, a flare a drape
      or a fuzz

why, talent could be alien DNA—the crack of a snare
by the lift shaft

    it's steely here
    where the lilt might relieve

partnered to stare, always on the dial
our town punches itself to sing

Nocturnal

i.m. Julian Bream

Strings vibrate in the hall, a spirit
with eyes squeezed shut and head bobbing
might be the strike of fingernails
through a backward telescope, pear-body
to belly as rings of colour float
restless in blackfaced night. A cockney always
between the power station and the dogs home
plucks for cash—it's done for yourself
even against the score and that's the way
to reach others. Cell to cell a smallish voice
breaks to put back winding figures
which wake in sleep and breath in death
tubed in narcotic joy.

Tower and Gravel-bed

'Yet something to the memory sticks at last'
for Stephen Gill

Tigers are wiser, says a bitumen script on the wall
in Brasenose Lane, while cells inside
studded with sentry boards and leaves
try to instruct. Wisteria almost wrapping the clock
might further sleep and seal loyalty
though new names on doors could jolt
any bottled mind and wake a painted prophet.

Does this light go out a guttering candle—or flash
a winding beam? Here on the stairs
where someone with city smoke can chuck
spoils and trophies we trace a grey, fretted border
where spires pierce the sky—needle
or pyramid—some spot from the land before
that now speaks ungravelled to show another way.

.

Obituary

My friend Gavin Selerie, who has died aged 73, was a writer whose collections of poetry included *Azimuth* (1984), *Roxy* (1996), *Le Fanu's Ghost* (2006) and *Hariot Double* (2016). He was born in Hampstead in 1949, the son of Peter Alexander Shaw Selerie, a wine merchant and World War II war-hero, and Muriel Selerie (*née* Lee). The Seleri family came to London from northern Italy around 1880 and ran a restaurant in Wardour Street. Muriel Lee worked for a film-company in Wardour Street before her marriage and also appeared in advertising films for Spectator Short Films.

Gavin was educated at Haleybury School, Lincoln College, Oxford, and the University of York, where he undertook research on Renaissance literature. In addition to his major books, *Azimuth* (1984), *Roxy* (1996), *LeFanu's Ghost* (2006), and *Hariot Double* (2016), he also published *Days of '49* (1999) with the poet and visual artist Alan Halsey (1949–2022); they collaborated with David Annwn and others on *Danse Macabre* (1997) and *The Canting Academy* (2008). Selerie favoured long forms, volume-length sequences conceived of as research projects, where original academic research was combined with formal inventiveness and a serious playfulness. *LeFanu's Ghost* was based on research into the complicated Sheridan and LeFanu families; *Hariot Double* brought together Gavin's wide-ranging knowledge of the Renaissance, his love of music and his fascination with London by juxtaposing the Renaissance polymath Thomas Hariot and the jazz saxophonist Joe Harriott. There were also shorter sequences such as *Elizabethan Overhang* (1989) and *Tilting Square* (1992); his *Collected Sonnets* were published by Shearsman Books in 2019. His work appeared in anthologies such as *The New British Poetry* (1988), *Other: British and Irish poetry since 1970* (1999) and the ground-breaking *Reality Street Book of Sonnets* (2008). *Music's Duel: New and Selected Poems, 1972–2008* (2009) collected some of his work.

Between 1979 and 1983, he conducted the *Riverside Interviews*, a series of book-length interviews with poets and playwrights (from Allen Ginsberg and Jerome Rothenberg through to Tom

McGrath). He published critical work on poetry beginning with a study of Charles Olson in 1980 and including two interviews with Ed Dorn (2013) and essays on Pound and contemporary poetry. He taught at the University of London Extra-Mural Department (later part of Birkbeck College) from the 1980s to 2004.

Gavin was diagnosed with glioblastoma in the autumn of 2022. He was able to complete his memoir of his time in the US during 1968 (*Edges of Memory*). He is survived by his partner, the poet Frances Presley, his sister Clare, a nephew, Peter, and a niece, Gemma.

ROBERT HAMPSON

Acknowledgements

The executors of Gavin Selerie's literary estate have endeavoured to identify online publication of the poems in this volume, and acknowledge earlier appearances in *Stride Magazine, Blackbox Manifold, Junction Box, Noon* and *Purge*.

'Line of What Make or Sort' appeared in *For the Future: Poems and Essays in Honour of J.H. Prynne on His 80th Birthday*, edited by Ian Brinton, Shearsman Books, 2016.

'S&G Variations' appeared in *Hilson, Hilson: the poetry of Jeff Hilson*, ed RTA Parker, Crater Press, 2020.

'Tower and Gravel-bed' appeared in a PDF eBook from Lincoln College, Oxford (2021), to celebrate 50 years of Stephen Gill's fellowship:
https://indd.adobe.com/view/a19d8d44-30e0-41b4-948c-7ce6f884c734